DOGGOLESCENCE

Poems by Kyra

(and Rachel Oates)

BUT MOSTLY KYRA!

ABOUT THE AUTHOR

Kyra is a 6 year old Staffordshire Bull Terrier who was adopted from Battersea Dogs & Cats Home on 11th April 2018.

She enjoys beef, playing ball, cuddles and long runs in the park.

She currently lives in London with her ~~servant~~ mum, Rachel.

You can follow her on Instagram @KyraTheStaffy

POOP

(inspired by Sleep)

I like poops! Poops are fun!

My pooping work is never done!

I like steak! Steak is great!

Anyone who hates it must be fake!

When I chase my ball around,

Everyone calls me a little clown!

Look, I know this poem is *really* dumb,

But it's better than what comes out of my bum.

Also, mate, I'm a dog.

What did you expect? Shakespeare?!

MINE

(inspired by Relative)

Your food is mine.

The bed is mine.

Your face is also mine.

MIRROR

(inspired by Cut)

There's another dog

in MY bedroom,

She staring at me with her beady eyes

and stupid ears.

"What are you looking at?"

I bark at her.

She tilts her head up and

Our eyes meet.

"What are you looking at?"

She mocks.

I stomp my paw and

refuse to give in.

"Go on, get out! Out!"

I growl in her face.

She does look kinda strong

I have to admit.

"Go on, get out! Out!"

She responds.

How dare she? This is

MY HOUSE.

"Alright," I warn her,

"You asked for this!"

I wiggle my bum and

Get ready to pounce...

I'm baring my teeth and

So is she!

I leap off the bed!

She jumps too.

My paws stretch out,

My mouth opens wide.

And my poor nose bangs

Into the mirror.

"Muuuuuuuum!"

I cry.

GIFTS

(inspired by Lotion)

Have you ever received a gift...

> **FOR ME?! THIS IS THE BEST!**

...That was placed inside a box...

> **OMG I LOVE OPENING BOXES**

...That was recycled from another,

Much more intriguing present?

> **WHAT? DID YOU SAY SOMETHING?**

> **I'M JUST FOCUSED ON THIS EXCITING BOX!**

Like, you pull back the pretty paper...

> **I'LL TEAR IT WITH MY PAWS**

...and you see iPad packaging

> **WHO CARES ABOUT THAT? MAYBE THIS IS A BALL?**

But then you open the lid

And inside...

OMG IT'S A BALL.

IT'S A BALL

IT'S A BALL

IT'S A BALL

FANK YOUUUUUUUU

PRETENDING TO BE BO BURNHAM

(inspired by Concealer)

I am loved because I love others.

I love others because I am loved.

STICKS (ARE GREAT BUT SO ARE YOU)

(inspired by Sticks)

You're a snack-bringer, cuddle-giver,

Toy-buyer, stick-finder.

A tall girl, my whole world.

My best friend 'till the end.

Receiver of my face licks, many sniffs,

And t' rest of my amazing gifts.

You're a poop-scooping tummy-rubber,

Head-scratching Kyra-lover.

You take care of me when I'm poorly,

Even love me when I'm naughty.

You're always think I'm smart and funny,

You're my snuggle-buddy and my mummy.

SAD

is bad.

No, but, like, really. It's bad.

No be sad human.

I'm here.

Look at my face.

I'll cheer you up.

(inspired by Sad)

POETRY

(inspired by Poetry)

I want to write you a poem but I'm not so good with words.

It's tough being a dog to make your voice feel heard.

But you know I really love you and want to make you art,

To show off to the whole world, the place you have in my heart.

I tried to make a painting but the canvas got too wet,

I couldn't help but dribble from the moment that we met.

I tried to take a photo but my paws, they don't have thumbs.

I don't even have a camera but I tried to borrow mum's.

And now you're gone forever, I'll never forget you,

But I can't help but think, this feels like deja vu.

I really couldn't help it, you made me drool and shake,

I'm sorry that I ate you, I just can't resist a steak.

QUOTES

(inspired by Quotes)

"Oh hey pretty girl!"

— *Someone I want to pet me*

"What's your name?!"

— *Someone I want to pet me*

"Oh gross, I hate dogs."

— *Someone I want to pet me*

"No really I'm scared of dogs. Please get it away"

— *Someone I want to pet me*

"Meow"

— *Trash*

DONATION

(inspired by O-Positive)

I donated poop today.

Feels good to leave my mark.

MY FAVOURITE THINGS

Chasing

And Snoring

Running

And Peeing

Bouncing

And Sleeping.

I am Pickle

And I am little.

SNIFF

(inspired by Iron)

Some time last week

My mum took out the bins

And I sniffed all the bags.

And I don't know,

I just felt like there's a snack in there somewhere.

BIRD

(inspired by Bird)

I saw him today, in MY garden

Strutting around, thinking he was a hard 'un.

Nah mate, this is Kyra's house!

I waggled my bum, stomped my paws

Bounced and pounced, leapt off all fours.

Caught his tail feathers in my mouth.

I spat them out and growled and grumbled,

I could tell that he was pretty humbled.

He knew I had him... nearly.

He'd lost his pride and flew away,

So we could play another day.

The fun's all in the chase, really.

BOYFRIEND

(inspired by Recess)

Kyra and Ronnie

Sitting in the park,

S-N-O-R-I-N-G!

First comes sleeping

Then comes bouncing,

And then I lick his butt to remind him,

I'M IN CHARGE HERE,

OK?!

IDOL

(inspired by Idol)

'Kyra, if you could trade lives with anyone who would it be?'

"NO ONE. I LOVE MY LIFE."

'Oh. Well I guess we can all learn something from that.'

stating the obvious is poetry now

TIME

(inspired by Time)
- From Rachel's perspective

Isn't is funny

How you can go your entire life

Without someone

Then one day

You go to Battersea

And realise

Your entire life

was leading up to

this moment.

What did I ever do without you Kyra?

HUMANS

(inspired by Pets and Continued)

Humans are weird. Dogs adopting humans is weird.

Think about it.

We could have anyone we wanted,

but we choose a certain human to love and care for us.

And we become best friends. Family.

They depend on us and all we ask is they fill our food bowl.

We move into their home and make it our own.

We teach them tricks like how to throw a ball.

We let them take our photographs and buy us toys.

We snuggle together, share secrets and

We can't believe it's possible to have a life so happy

Together.

We trust each other, support each other, love each other.

Our love is pure, unconditional, unrivalled

And yet one day, as much as we don't want to, we have to go.

To leave them

All alone.

I'm sorry.

GONE

(inspired by Gone)

I don't fear death.

I fear leaving you all alone.

Who will look after you when I'm gone?

WISH

(inspired by Wish)

If I had one wish... IT WOULD BE FOR A LIFETIME SUPPLY OF BALLS, STEAK AND CUDDLES PLEASE THANK YOU.

OPINIONS

(inspired by Desperate)

I like people like I like my food:

It's all great but some are more great than others.

Also some make me vomit.

I'LL HELP

(inspired by Catholic)

"Mum, are you giving up anything for lent?"

'Kyra, we're atheists'

"Oh."

'You look disappointed.'

"Oh no.. I mean.. No..."

'Kyra? Talk to me Pickle.'

"It's just... I thought maybe you'd want to give up steak?"

'I don't eat steak anyway.'

"...or cheese? Or carrots?! OR CHICKEN?!"

'Why do you want me to give up so many foods, Bean?'

"No reason..."

...

"Well it's just... I thought maybe if you weren't eating them... I could eat them instead? You know, TO HELP."

FREE

(inspired by Rich)

My mamma calls me Small Bean,

But I know I am The Queen,

She feeds, loves and pets me,

And takes me out to go pee

We always run round on the green.

PHILOSOPHY

(inspired by Philosophy)

If I eat an entire pizza by myself in the woods,

And no one's around to see it...

Do you still think mum will clean up my poop for me?

FEELS

(inspired by Fashion)

I've always worn my heart on my paws

And love on my face.

Without a doubt, you could read my mood,

From the wagging of my tail

Or the tilt of my head,

The bounce in my step or the shuffle in my stride,

My feelings all out there, never implied.

Some people hide their feelings away,

Covering everything up.

They hide what they want with silence or words,

Etiquette rules are like hiding in baggy clothes.

I stay naked.

You know what I want from the tone of my cry:

Pee, drink or snack, or a sleepy sigh.

I don't see the point in faking or lying,

I am who I am.

No point in denying I'm the goodest girl

And asking means getting.

Rules are there to be broken.

Why don't humans get that?

SOUL MATE

(inspired by Fate)

My soul mate is an angel.

He's small but strong and never leaves my side.

He's smooth and resilient and always bounces back.

No matter where he goes, I follow.

At night we lay in bed and I whisper to him 'I will always find you'.

He's an all-round gem and I'd call him my best friend.

I love his soft skin and rosy glow, even his curves and cracks and imperfections.

Oh BALL I do love you.

But I've heard humans say opposites attract so what does that say about me?

Ahh who cares?! I'm perfect too.

HONEY

(inspired by Flies)

They told me, "you'd catch more flies with honey."

But I don't want to catch flies.

I'd rather eat the honey.

FALLING OVER

(inspired by Match)

Sometimes you need to pick yourself up,

Get your mum to brush you off,

Check your paws and lick your nose,

And ask yourself,

'Ok... now where did my ball go?'

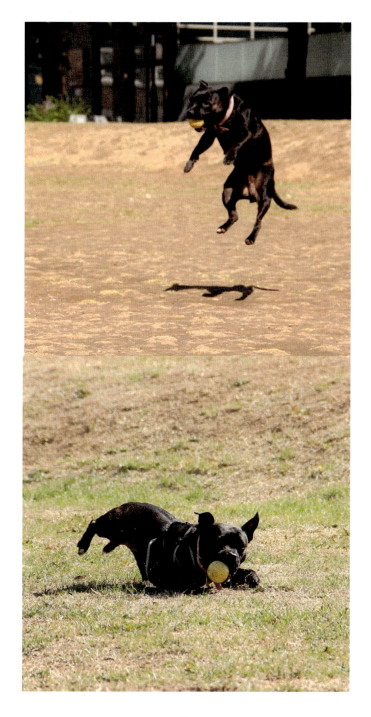

NIGHTS

Nights in Battersea were cold as hell.

    They gave us blankets and toys

    A bed and a space of my own

    But I slept alone.

Concrete under my paws,

Lights out with no one to snuggle,

A pillow that wasn't mine,

A bowl of water, borrowed.

    Other dogs barking, crying, snoring, waiting

    And I was left alone.

Nights with you are warm and safe.

    We snuggle in our bed.

    I tuck myself between your legs,

    Or round your head,

    Or, my favourite, in your arms.

A soft pillow under my head,

My nose buried in your neck.

Paws and arms and legs and hearts,

A tangled, interwoven blanket.

       I dribble on your shoulder, snore in your ear.

       You kiss my little head and whisper in my ear,

'Sleep well little one, you'll never be alone

       again.'

STICK HUNT

We're going on a stick hunt!

I hope we find a big one!

To throw and chase,

To hunt and race,

I'll catch that stick, you'll see!

We're going on a stick hunt!

I hope we find a long one!

To chew and break,

To bend and shake,

I'll munch on him, you'll see!

We're going on a stick hunt!

I hope we find a new one!

To carry back home,

To the stick-free zone,

I'll sneak him inside, you'll see!

TEXTS

(inspired by K)

Messages | **Mama** | **Contact**

6:06 PM

> HEY

> HEY MUM

> WHEN YOU COMING HOME???

> YOU'VE BEEN GONE FOR SO LONG.

6:07 PM

> OMG!!! MUM COME HOME!!!

> EMERGENCY

> SOS

Messages — **Mama** — **Contact**

> PLEASE

> MUM

> I LOST MY BALL UNDER THE SOFA AND IT'S GONE FOREVER

> WHAT AM I GOING TO DO?!!?

> MUUUUUM!

> oh

> nevermind

> it rolled out again

| 3 | 6:09 PM | 50 % |

Messages **Mama** Contact

6:08 PM

sigh

STILL MISSING YOU

do do do...

WHAT?

OH NOTHING.

JUST SINGING TO MYSELF BECAUSE YOU'RE NOT HERE TO HEAR IT

WELL THIS MUST BE IT

ALL ALONE FOREVER

Text Message   Send

3	6:09 PM	50 %
Messages	**Mama**	Contact

> I'VE BEEN ABANDONED

> I'M AN ORPHAN AGAIN

> I SEE HOW IT IS

6:09 PM

> THAT'S IT

> I'M PEEING ON THE BED.

> NO WAIT I'M JOKING.

> YOU KNOW I'D NEVER DO THAT

> I'M A GOOD GIRL

Text Message   Send

| vodafone | 6:10 PM | 50 % |

Messages **Mama** **Contact**

> PLS COME HOME

> MUM?!

> I MISS YOU

> ARE YOU BRINGING SNACKS BACK?

> OR A NEW BALL?

> THAT MUST BE IT!!

6:10 PM

> OR NOT

Messages — **Mama** — **Contact**

> APPARENTLY YOU JUST DON'T LOVE ME ANYMORE

> I SEE...

Kyra.

I'm taking the bins out.

I've been gone 4 minutes.

> 4 MINUTES TOO LONG

I love you Smoogs.

> love you too

ABOUT THIS BOOK

I'm not going to pretend this is a book I've spent years working on and carefully crafting, because it's not. I did put a surprising amount of work into it though and I've ended up with something I'm strangely proud of.

It started as a joke between me and fellow Youtuber, *Alizee*, when I told her 'we should make a video where Kyra writes poetry!' Even this idea wasn't original though, I was inspired by *SuperRaeDizzle's* video where she got her dog to choose her art supplies (to draw a portrait of him, of course!). And these ideas only came together after I critiqued *Gabbie Hanna*'s... interesting 'poetry' collection *Adultolescence* in a short series of videos.

In those videos I tried to critique Gabbie's poems constructively, for the most part anyway. What did I like? What did Gabbie do well? What were her flaws? Which bits seemed lazy or undeveloped? How could she improve them? And, of course, I compared her poetry to other poems which I thought she could learn something from – poems of a similar theme or which tried to use similar techniques to Gabbie.

These videos performed far better than I ever expected and the feedback was overwhelming and lovely but a recurring joke I spotted in the comments was 'I wrote better poetry than this at X age'. My silly brain wanted to respond with the joke: 'Oh yeah, I bet my 6 year old daughter could write better poetry... and she's DOG!'

And so everything started come together and I had my idea... I would craft some (terrible) poems mad-libs style and get Kyra to fill in the blanks by choosing words off cards.

This proved way harder to plan than I first thought but after a few hours and many Kyra cuddles later, we were just about ready to film a video creating 5 or so poems. Except I had an idea...

I'd actually really enjoyed creating these 'poems' for Kyra but what if I tried to make some of Gabbie's poems better? Or what if I could at least change them to highlight the flaws, for educational purposes of course... and who am I kidding, for parody and giggles too!

So a few hours work turned into... well, many hours work. I was up late and night writing and rewriting and having fun and being silly. I wanted to try and capture Kyra's fun, child-like, innocent but loving voice (which I imagine she has based on her facial expressions) in each poem. I wanted her excitement, happiness, love of fun and just general contentment with life.

Gabbie's poems were a great starting point. Some poems like *Honey* and *Wish* were more heavily influenced than others – I took the same structure and a few of the same lines and thought 'well how would Kyra respond to this? She doesn't care about being seen as 'deep' or 'intellectual' all she wants is to enjoy herself and be happy...' and that's how those 2 poems were born.

Other poems I changed more considerably; I only took an image or idea and crafted a whole new poem around them. This was the case for *Birds* – a poem about chasing birds, one of Kyra's favourite things to do. And *Feels* – an attempt at a poem about how humans spend to much time hiding their feelings, pretending to feel or think things they don't. It's like a person hiding their body under baggy clothes so you can't really see what they look like. As a dog, Kyra is the opposite – she has no clothes to hide behind and, similarly, she never hides any of her feelings. For this one I tried to follow Gabbie's basic structure but then I thought 'hang on, this poem is about saying screw it to formal rules and expressing yourself...' so I broke out of the rules and structure I'd set for myself at the end.

Other poems like *Nights* were completely original and only inspired by many wonderful night snuggled up in bed with my little Karoo.

I don't know how well or or any of my intentions came across in this collection. I am not a poet. Not by any stretch of the imagination. But I am a dog lover, a very enthusiastic pawrent, and I at least attempt to be an entertainer and educator. Let's not comment on my success there...

You can watch the video where Kyra writes her poems on my Youtube channel: **youtube.com/racheloates**

Or you can follow us on social media:

@Rachel0ates

@KyraTheStaffy

But for now, thank you for supporting this silly little project of mine, I cannot tell you how much fun I had and how much I appreciate all your love and support.

Thank you and I'll see you all again very soon!

— Rachel Oates

xxx

Made in the USA
Monee, IL
09 June 2021